Feather Silence

Feather Silence

Ben Murnane

A. & A. Farmar

© Ben Murnane 2010

All rights reserved. No part of this publication may be reproduced in any form or by any means without the prior permission of the publisher or else under the terms of a licence permitting photocopying issued by the Irish Copyright Licensing Agency or a similar reproductive rights organisation.

British Library Cataloguing in Publication Data
A CIP catalogue record for this book is available from the British Library

ISBN: 978-1-906353-24-7

This edition first published in 2010
by
A. & A. Farmar Ltd
78 Ranelagh Village, Dublin 6, Ireland
Tel +353-1-496 3625 Fax +353-1-497 0107
Email afarmar@iol.ie Website: www.aafarmar.ie

Printed and bound by Gemini
Typeset and designed by A. & A. Farmar

*To my parents, Mai and Des,
for too many things to list*

Contents

Foreword Eamon Grennan   9

Michael	13
A swan in summer	14
Sunroom	16
Outside porch, image	17
The common room	19
About to begin	20
Between Killiney and Dalkey	21
September (side effect)	22
North & South	23
Christmas	24
Hidden	25
Dreams are the streets I walk	26
Shanaveagh again	27
The rhododendrons seem more alive this year	28
DART route	30
At work	32
Ordinary	33
Feathersoft	34
Psychiatric ward	35
Studying in hospital waiting rooms	36
Dancer	37
Through the raindrops	38
Writing	41
The house near Renvyle	42
Puddles	43
Swans	44
Harbour variations	45
My birthday	46
So much	47

CONTENTS

Skylight	48
Synaesthetic	49
Monkstown by night	50
Deep	51
Rain across landscapes	53
Write a poem	54
Hair colour	55
Hotel room window	56
Waiting after school	57
The nerve girl	58
Grief	60
Summer	61
The loss of you	62
Absence	63
When you lay in the long grass	64
The young couple beside me	65
White umbrella	66
Trinity College/January morning	67
The days	68
Up and down wildly	69
Saw the river run away with the moonlight	70
His destination	71
Perspective	72
Songs about pianos	73
Possibilities	74
The idea of autumn	75
Walk	76
Memory of dancing	77
Notes	79

Foreword

What I especially like and admire about my friend Ben's poems is the way in which—with neither self-pity nor self-dramatisation—they allow the life of a young man moving through the world, carrying the weight of almost unspeakable illness, to be seen in its real, its ordinary colours. 'Almost unspeakable illness', I say, since it has been spoken with courage and literary panache in Ben's own memoir, *Two in a Million*. Because they mostly ignore the facts of his illness, these poems may be read as a curious shadowing of the memoir—insisting that his life be seen from a different, a more, let's say, quotidian angle.

Formally simple, the poems compose a portrait of this young man experiencing (physically, emotionally, thoughtfully) the normal bothers of his age. They embody his lyric love of a western landscape, and track his observant eye moving around his home base in Dublin, his life as a college student, his cultural enthusiasms, his travails as a lover. Exemplary and emblematic of a youthful romanticism, at their best they have a little something of the simplicity of the early Kavanagh: the same sort of vulnerability, the same sort of rapt wonder, the same emotional honesty finding expression through a non-showy, heartfelt voice. 'Outside porch', indeed, even reminds me in its simple lyrical descriptions of Kavanagh's great later poem, 'The Hospital'. Ben writes:

> I don't know what you'd call this place.
> An outside porch.
>
> Under Perspex, between two doors—
> one leads to the kitchen,
> the other to
> a sort of nowhere.

Rain on the Perspex, looks like
I'm looking up from under a river,
water U-ing along.

The long grass ahead is striped, yellow and green—
like the sun and the clouds striping themselves
on the mountains here:
a layer of gold then a layer of shadow.

Rain hides itself in the grass.

'Naming these things', as Kavanagh says in 'The Hospital',
   'is the love-act and its pledge;
For we must record love's mystery without claptrap,
Snatch out of time the passionate transitory.'

   I think Ben, in his own way, is trying to get at 'love's mystery without claptrap', and the best of his poems bear witness to a threatened consciousness (call it body and spirit) trying to mark the moments, the occasions, of its own sense-life and thought-life, to give these moments of apprehension—whether of love or landscape or (especially in the pieces celebrating Michael Jackson) cultural awareness—their due.
   What's especially impressive—given, as *Two in a Million* demonstrates, the facts of a horrendous illness being overcome 'without claptrap' by a species of courage and patience few of us are ever asked to display—is how normal the emotional and observing life of this young man, this young writer, actually is. Emotionally direct, with 'the ordinariness/all hearts/demand', the poems in *Feather Silence*, aside from their value as poems, are also fascinating documents in a remarkable journey of survival, testaments in every line to a brave, unbowed, enduring heart—anchored in the ordinary world, yet not afraid to dream. As he says in 'Writing':

> some books about America
> on my bed,
> and a dozen pages of raw,
> still-bleeding work.
> A swig of something, a glance at
> private inspiration.
> My dreams are somewhere
> here.

And here, indeed—the dreams, the daily life, the loves, the beloved places—they are.

Eamon Grennan

Michael

All I know of you is that
you've wandered in the rain,
with those feet like little universes

and a face white as a void. Michael—
they fashioned you a star, and
then snatched it away.

A swan in summer

I
Summer is an awful time
to be in college and be alone,
when spring's new beginning has fizzled
like a sick magic trick—
its dawn of budding daffodils
gone.

Now everything's dry
and too hot.

On the grass
so many bronze-skinned bodies buzz
like bees on honeycomb, and
kiss as though they could
suck love's essence out of one another.

II
I go up to the Green, sit
weary beneath its canopy of leaves
snatching the day's glory.
But the scene is no better:

Happy couples and squabbling ones
flash by in untouchable soap-opera images,
and I envy them all.

A SWAN IN SUMMER

Yet my eyes twitch, there's
something—yes,
I see him now:

a swan
drifting white as a cloud across the sky of the lake—
proud and nonchalant
as some kind of champion . . .

I'd like to be that swan.

Sunroom

In summer I like to sit in our sunroom
and watch
the old-fashioned lilac:
she dresses so well.

The cherry blossoms
are always
dusted like sugar
over the tarmac; the clouds
are white camellias, blooming
on the sky.

And as the sun bows out, she
makes the evening
her
Mexican gold poppy.

I go back to my reading, the colours
warm and soft
against my heart.

Outside porch, image

I

I don't know what you'd call this place.
An outside porch.

Under Perspex, between two doors—
one leads to the kitchen,
the other to
a sort of nowhere.

Rain on the Perspex, looks like
I'm looking up from under a river,
water U-ing along.

The long grass ahead is striped, yellow and green—
like the sun and the clouds striping themselves
on the mountains here:
a layer of gold then a layer of shadow.

Rain hides itself in the grass.

II

An outside porch—smoker's porch, writer's porch;
writing smoker's porch.

Writing is always
pulling the cigarette out of the packet;
you think one day you'll get to light it
but you don't.
And you keep pulling because it seems so easy
and so maybe.

OUTSIDE PORCH, IMAGE

The static of rain hitting things;
thousands of little noises,
thousands of ending droplets.

There are so many theatres
in this house.
Like the back patio that
the birds come to
in pairs in the morning—they feed
each other and toss grubs and pull out
bits of weeds with their beaks;
I watch them from the living room.
Or the window that the moths,
those little flapping triangles,
come to when it's dark—they won't stop
thudding towards the light.

It's nine-thirty a.m., and I haven't
been to sleep yet.

Just
keep
working
these days. It's good.

Rain greys everything
ahead.

I don't know what you'd call this place.
The outside porch of dreaming.

The common room

Art that's wild colour caged in glass,
a candle with the Virgin Mary,
and blue curtains lapping like sea-waves
in the breeze;

photos of the not-forgotten,
two-tone green walls, and your hands
dashing over the piano keys like perfect animals—

every note
swelling in the room till it touches my skin.

'Do you remember this one?'

About to begin

It's about to begin—this 'new world',
this 'new start', these 'best years',
but oh,
I don't want them;

I want to hide in memory
and never find my dreams in all their
blinding glimmer;

I want to fear tomorrow and never
let go of the waiting,
on this train journey
I hope never ends.

Between Killiney and Dalkey

Have you ever seen the sun get caught
in the train windows,
between Killiney and Dalkey?

Like a cobweb of light, the
scratches on the glass
glow
orange or yellow or red,

depending on the morning.
And even though it's stuck
in the window, the sun

still hangs over the sea
like a tablet
about to fall
into a cup
and set all the water fizzing.

September (side effect)

I see the world through my window,
where a purple sun drips
into the spoon of a moon,
and people drown and live.

A child is screaming but I can't help,
because I broke every bone in my body
some time ago, and
towers are tumbling around me
on television screens.

A secret agent arrives, and tells me to remember
words—'world', 'watch', 'blue'. Jesus,
my life's in peril,

and they pick today
to let me
begin.

North & South

I didn't know people could
be so small,
like tiny black exclamation marks
falling onto a new page.

Lives caught in glass,
and metal and concrete
and the sun of a day
that shouldn't have been that sunny.

Christmas

Tiny spheres of rain
caught on these knobbly branches—
small Christmas baubles
in February.

Hidden

What I like about Ireland
is the weather—it's like an old man
that has his moods
that change so many times
in a day,
but he won't change.

Memory:
the leaves of that branch
skirting the water
the way your hand
did
brings back
fingertips
cold in the flow
but a smile still
'cause it's what you wanted,
just fun:
a brush with the river.

I like it here, even with
the memories.
I can see things in the landscape
no one else does,
things that happened.
I like it here.

Dreams are the streets I walk

Dreams are the streets I walk,
while sleeping or awake; streets
that cry like abandoned children,
and their tears fall softly on my lap,
these little droplets of tomorrow.

Shanaveagh again

I
I'm on this bridge again,

smoke tumbling
from my mouth,

yet now ash falls
as nothing more than ash:

grey swirling through
heavy grey.

II
The stillness of the air
is taut like canvas;

the river's trickles
streaking through it

are my lines of paint:

I'm making
watercolours.

III
The night, it drips like oil
over the bushes;

and a daddy longlegs rises
on a tide to the stars.

But I go inside to write,
because

inspiration is momentary.

The rhododendrons seem more alive this year

The rhododendrons seem more alive
this year.

I come here to write.
I think that if I can just find something
to say
to the world, the world
won't sit on me
the way it seems to
so often
now.

The rhododendrons seem
more alive
this year, purple flowers
bunched in lumpy hemispheres
on thick bushes.

I spend my days wanting to walk.
But, by the time
I've finished what I want to finish, the sun has
plopped itself down
between the hills.
It gives an orange yawn
and that's it; business closed, sorry.

Morning comes and as usual
I'm looking for poems
in the water.
There's a stagnant bit, where green gunk gathers,
while all the other brown trickles
swim giddily
downstream.
Giddy water, swimming trickles . . .
I've got a line
now, something
to play with.

Blue
from the dawn
rushes to touch everything
in sight;
my cigarette juts from my lips.

DART *route*

Between Killiney and Dalkey, the train
arcs its way
along the cliff
over the sea;
sometimes there's a craggy shore
below, sometimes
the sea hides it, pulling itself down
like a blind.

Here, the horizon yawns,
wide,
till it reaches the lips
of both Bray
and Howth:
the whole DART route,
it's a gaping mouth
of possibilities.

Far from my train window, ships
swim into the sky: a sky
painted so differently
on different days—
orange-soaked,
pink with flamingo-feather clouds,
polished blue, or
grey as a face near death.

DART ROUTE

I see them every morning,
this sea and its sky;
after their act, my train chugs
towards tunnels and stations ... and
the sea and the sky
go off together, hand in hand,
towards someplace
unseen.

At work

I'm sitting there,
captured by you at work. It's August, and the sun
touches our skin like the warmest hands;
your mural sparkles with drying paint, the colours
nauseating in their beauty.

Something about your cut grey rags,
the paint in your hair,
makes you just leak sex.
But you're shifting roles like an effortless actor—
one moment on the ground,
a little girl playing with her paints;
the next up the ladder:
a Master again, curling a lizard's tongue in a sun.

Suddenly the waitress comes with our coffee,
and you rest to read the foam like tea leaves.
A brown twist in mine reminds you of a love-flame.
'You're going to have a mad passionate love life',
you predict. Then

you glance at the murk of your cup.
'I'm going to fall down a bog hole', you laugh.
'Till Ben comes to rescue me.'

I can't say anything;
I'm captured by you at work.

Ordinary

And then
they began to talk
in those
familiar tones,
intimate
because they are
ordinary;

they became
ordinary
to each other—
not
'dull'
ordinary,
but
'so-much-a-part-of-each-other's-lives'
ordinary:

the ordinariness
all hearts
demand.

Feathersoft

Their hands
are gliding over one another's—

feathersoft dancers
of attraction;

lightly sexual, subtle and striking
as a pirouette:

the easy grace
of a love beginning.

Psychiatric ward

The television is always on:
speaking even
when no one listens.

There is too much space
for thought. Only cigarettes
light up the boredom,

and they don't do it
very well. Dressing gowns
without their belts

lie on empty couches; pyjamas
soak up the blood
of cuts

that won't stay closed. And a
trembling girl, she

waits

waits

waits

for her evening
hot chocolate.

Studying in hospital waiting rooms

It feels like I've been sitting here
all the time I've sat;
in one hand there's something from school
or later college, in the other
something from hospital—
a form for blood tests, probably.

The seats change—
they've been brown plastic
and curvy metal
and wooden
with furry bits in the middle;

but the sitting's been the same.
Rooms for waiting in hospitals, places to study
enzymes or Frost
or Orientalism.

I don't think words like 'postmodern'
go beside 'full blood count'.
I can't put rings
on the fingers of the things
in my two hands
and marry them.

I learned in hospital that school
didn't go there.

Dancer

I remember being
so moved by him, by
his being who he is,
the sheerness of his voice
climbing somewhere in soft words,
skipping nothing human,
loving that he could love.

Night skies moved with his feet, stars
pocketing themselves
in and out of the stage lights:
the wonder of socks,
silver glint
sparkle
wink
twirl:
glitter moments.

But—

There were times when he slowed,
curled over
like he wanted a shell.
He wanted us to smile and cry
for him.
Part of the act.

Through the raindrops

A voice
I couldn't see
called my name.

The sky was what you noticed
then: a sky
heavy with itself,
like
a man and his secrets.

The clouds
made
everything beneath them
grey.

I was so far
from hands that knew me,
but every eye I passed
seemed to think
that I was theirs.

I saw only the sky,
and the life
the city
held to itself, the way a mother
holds the child
she needs.

A man
in a suit
watches a pigeon
ignore him;

THROUGH THE RAINDROPS

a woman's coffee
waterfalls from her cup
onto the smooth tiles
of a coffee shop floor;

a baseball
pulls a shattered window
with it,
as it spins into
an abandoned apartment.

Then,

rain—
like shards
of glass,
soft shards
that melt in your hair.

People
lifted their faces
to catch the pieces
of the breaking sky;

little bits of it
were tumbling over me.

On and on and on it came, while
the man in the suit
moved his head back
and let his eyelids fall;

while the woman left
her spilt coffee, stood
on a soaked roadway, and
held her arms out;

while the boy
with the baseball bat
watched his clothes
gather the wet.

A little bit of the sky
ran down my face
today, when
I was a stranger
in this city, just hoping

the world
wouldn't lose me
through the raindrops.

Writing

Cigarette butts and a dormant
lighter,
Caffeine Free Diet Coke
and scattered CDs.
The World Cup in the
background,
some books about America
on my bed,
and a dozen pages of raw,
still-bleeding work.
A swig of something, a glance at
private inspiration.
My dreams are somewhere
here.

The house near Renvyle

I'm standing on the bridge
over our big stream,
or small river, the water

gushing in my ears, billowing
and stagnating around rocks
clustered in islands. Ash
from my last cigarette

falls in hot snowflakes
onto dew-kissed grass, smoke
caresses the rain ...

I flick the brown butt into
the soaked bushes, and crunch
a path back to the cottage, my mind
heavy with words.

Puddles

The rain has left itself
in places where
it can hold the light
for me—

puddles of orange-pink; bright water
keeping the night
from covering itself
too much:

the ends of electricity,
flickering with breeze-made ripples.
Maybe, perhaps memories
are held like that:

softly by us—
reflected light,
humming in so many pools
at once.

They make my walk easier:
the stars aren't talking
to the moon, and the trees
are too silent and black;

I'm left to follow
the glowing puddles home,
and to hope
they know the way.

Swans

I take this bus every day;
each journey is a dig
to find something I can use
in a poem. Today, we pass by
the Dargle River, and

the swans have wrapped themselves
into oval packages; they've
folded themselves up
like portable appliances. Their
white necks meander over
their soft backs. Beaks are tucked
under wings.

Like magnified snowflakes,
they spin so slowly
on the river,
softly upsetting
the summer water. And I marvel
at what a poem
that could make.

Harbour variations

You should have seen
the waves today:
little bobbing triangles

flowed and spiked;
they were
an intimate fabric,

with spots of sun
sewn in—here,
smooth as the back

of a child's hand; there,
wrinkled
like an old man's cheeks.

At once, they were speckled
with raindrops, and
spitting from against the rocks.

You should have seen them,
living like that,
on this dying winter's day.

My birthday

All blue suit and new shoes,
left worry to stray:
turned to you to
take me home.

Our steps stir fallen
leaves, thoughts of
blackcurrant tang,
Wicklow views ...
 ... Our beginning.

All blue suit and new shoes,
drunk and cold;
turned to you to take me home.
You did.

So much

Across the table, behind
glasses, you,
beauty so wild.

You're so full of
time, bustling over yourself
like hurrying insects, carrying
each moment
to its burst. Each moment
bursts on you
like you are
a canvas
for the last great paintings.

You see—you always
make me lose myself
in clichés about love.

Skylight

I keep my stars in
a box above my bed, my
special white pin-tips.

Synaesthetic

What colour
does a trombone sound like,
when it moves between
its deep blues?

She knows. She sees

its heavy rivers
running through
the pink splashes
of a piano's high notes;

above the instruments
the colours churn
for her:

the purple brushstrokes
of a cello
are thrust onto
the air, a canvas;

the yellow butterflies
of a flute
are so weightless

for the woman
who can see
the way music
weaves its rainbow.

Monkstown by night

Sometimes, he can be found
at his wooden desk
that's lined with papers:
his endless work;

out the window, to his right, the
cherry blossoms kiss: two trees
grow so close
they embrace each other.

Then, sometimes, he's at the window
in the next room, tea
heating his hands; he stands,
watching the streetlights

admire themselves
in puddles: their glow swims, its colour
somewhere between orange
and white.

Deep

I

Winter fades in
on pink skies, hanging over
the city lights.

Those city lights:
white, orange
and stammering red—

eyes
so the cars can see.

II

Now, it's dark before
you've walked the pier
in the afternoon;

the sea
sounds like
it's inside
your own head:

this settling
and unsettling
of water.

*

The stars slip themselves
into the pockets
of the clouds.

These days,
winter fades in
on pink skies, melting

into a moon

that's bright
and deep
as a life.

Rain across landscapes

I
Memories are clouds:
just white

that hides
the blue of dying seconds ...

II
they shift,
like rain across landscapes,

watering with tears
the places I tried to stay.

Write a poem

'Write a poem', she says,
like it's a cure-all for ills of the heart.
Thoughts, emotions flying
like objects thrown across my room;
it's a summer cocktail
with Molotov added.

Given a day, I would change
all the world. But I have
only this page
to share my wishes with. And
she says 'Write a poem'.

And it's not that I wouldn't.
The magic that happens
when I'm alone in my secrets
is maybe just illusion,
but I love it.

'Write a poem', she says, as if
it's a cure-all for ills of the heart.
It's just that writing a poem
is like falling off a log
—it hurts.

Hair colour

Dreams like balloons
up to the sun.

Those words too hard to
say, too long to say
I live because of you.

A flood of feelings, washed
out with your hair colour
in the shower.

Hotel room window

The sun a red
disc, some holiday
decoration in the sky.

Lights speckled in the
grass as the moon
takes over; the fountain
stops its gushing.

I turn from my
hotel room window, let
the curtain slide closed.

Waiting after school

Passing me by: a
flood of synthetics and
hairbands—the rush-hour
home-time blur.

Then there you
were. My nerves
shaking; my lips
on your cheek: in
a blink it's over.

Hardly a memory
now. But it was
my Everest
that day.

The nerve girl

It's years now
since her dreams rolled away
like broken yo-yos.

Today she sits
in an Italian café,
where the walls feel
close,

like her too-tight skin.

And she's fidgeting:
her thumbs are at work
on a coffee cup,

snapping its plastic top
and tearing the paper.

So, a drifting string on her coat
may be next,
or a little sachet of sugar:

no object is safe
from those scurrying fingers,
busy as termites.

But,
don't say a word,
for these hands
are not yours to judge:

THE NERVE GIRL

her hands,
they once belonged
on piano keys,

and oh,
how she could make thin air
orgasm.

Grief

Coffin silence. The coffin
is the epicentre of the silence
that shakes tears
from those here: little diamonds
from stone:
the hardness of any grief.

It's so neat,
the church:
concentric rings of people:
the nearest to you were the closest to you.

*

At the grave, I think you would have liked it,
we could see ourselves
in the varnish
of the coffin—bars of light
caught in the grooves
were spearing our reflected heads: You and the light
playing on your coffin,
you were killing us!

Summer

We lay back,
apart in our grief,
that day

when the tarmac was
a black hole
that might suck us into nothing,

and the sky was empty of answers.

*

There we were,
like corpses,
flattening little hills of hay

by the roadside;

and I wanted to tell you
how there were caverns inside me, and
if I could only hold you
till your body filled them.

*

I wished I could die,
just to see what it's like
and know if I'd want to stay.

The loss of you

It sinks in me
every day,

it sinks
like bodies in quicksand:

the loss of you.
It moves through me
so inevitably

and
so
slow...

Sometimes I think
it's an animal,
prowling over my organs
with heavy paws.

I ask it,
'What's left after heartbreak,
friend?'

And it tells me
there's nothing.

Absence

This pillow
might be your skin
that was like a dream-rest
to me;

and this room
might be your soul, inside which
I felt
smaller than a raindrop,

and yet
a part of the rain. Being
beside you
was like

seeing the world from space,
or
waiting by this window
for a day

that won't come,
my eyes
blindfolded
with stars.

When you lay in the long grass

You were sandwiched
between
the white bread-clouds
and the white houses
below.

The gorse
on our cliff
that day
was a mango yellow;

the wind
made the heather
a liquid purple, trickling
this way
then the other.

While you lay in the long grass, a rock
became my stool.

(I was perched
over the pools of your heart
like a bird
scanning a lake
for a fish ...

and I was jealous
of the flower
that was touching your skin.)

The young couple beside me

It's amazing the way
the branches of the trees bend towards the lake
like giraffes' necks,
till their leaves are almost drinking the water.

I'm on my bench in the Green,
and the young couple beside me are stopping and starting
a conversation about themselves,
her leg draped over his, her hair falling about her face
like autumn.

Far away, cranes stripe the horizon—shaping this city.
My couple are shaping togetherness.
His hand is fastened to hers
for safety,

while the ducks plop their heads beneath the brown ripples,
and jostle for breadcrumbs.

White umbrella

The branches
of the tree above
are
dropping down
over me
from the sky
like
a white umbrella.
Behind me, the sea's hands
are
slipping up
a stony beach,
long fingers
finding
every crack;
I can't watch them
slide down
and not think
of your groans.
Today, summer
hangs from the trees
like
an excess of tinsel. Bray Head
is
a swollen blister, a
little
infected
memory-blister. I'm here,
under
the soft arms
of flowers
on branches, just looking
for a needle.

Trinity College / January morning

The frost on the lawn
seems to reach into the air,
till the air is white,
too;

behind the branches
of the stripped cherry trees,
and behind
the ivy-clad railings,

the traffic moves
as though it should be
someplace else.

(In this chill,
the library looks good
to me.)

The days

The days when your lips
emptied into mine
ran from me, like you.

(Your spider-leg fingers
now scuttle up
another's arm.)

My hand taps the table
between us. I need to cover
the sound of my heart,

still rippling with
the nearness of your skin,
though your eyes look away.

Up and down wildly

Line across my sight;
night butterfly juts
in the air like
the final spikes before a flatline:
up and down wildly
above the soaked stones,
rain through everything,

everything is a colander
to the rain:
it finds holes
to get you.

A moth caught in smoke, wings
grey as thunder-clouds.
Now is no time for butterflies.
In the night, you can't even see the grey.

I said to the night butterfly,
'I'm sorry for my smoke.'
A cigar that's dead,
only black now
from the outside in, but I can still
feel the warmth
here
and here
and
here—

hidden in the dull cylinder
something burns:
possible head rush
coming.

Saw the river run away with the moonlight

Saw the river run away with the moonlight.
Don't know where they were going.
They made soft trickles
as they left me.

I pass the puddles that the stars
drop into—little shivering firefly-stars;
cold, drowning stars.
Rippling-with-splashes stars.

It's getting harder to pretend that the rain is
your skin
touching me.

His destination

There are nights that I have trouble going to sleep:
nights that move in and out of me
like ghosts;

hollow nights that yawn like caverns.

Often I'm at the window—and yes,
the North Star flickers—something—I remember—that's
fate winking.

Hollow nights that chill
like ghosts,
but hum beneath a glistening sky.

Perspective

I was never good with parties.
There were always legs
that pricked V-shaped fantasies—

oh dear,
I'm like an old man now,
'These young people', etc.

But apart was my zone—
there'd be spilt beer
and intoxicating music and bodies
so close they were inside each other,

but I'd wish for invisibility
till a friend'd say
'You're not part of the furniture, Ben',

'cause I needed reminding.

Songs about pianos

They rise in my mind,
these songs about pianos,
like ships on a lonely tide—
because

she used offer me crescendos
in evenings emptied of light,
with a trickle of keys
and rivers of Mozart or Dvorak;

each note was a pearl
fashioned by her fingertips
and hanging 'round my neck
like the weight of love I felt.

But now songs about pianos
are the closest I get
to those times when her hands
washed worry from my shore.

Now, each night,
the waves of the moon lap
against ivory that's silent,
and still as a memory.

Possibilities

English class, Plath
buzzing in my ear like
a familiar strangeness.

Three weeks before the end
of school, a faraway
aeroplane rolling on
the cotton-wool clouds
through my window.

Caught between the quiet past
and the unseen tomorrow,
days thudding slowly to
completion.

The idea of autumn

I wrote about this once before.
Or more than once.
All my poems are you,

your blood and mine,
our children.

I know,
if we were seasons, well,
you'd be summer—

all that sun
splashing in your smile;

and me, I'd be winter:
cold and quiet, like
a dying thing.

But the idea of autumn, that's
one which intrigues me:
between us, a meeting point—

a place where fruit falls,
where shivering gold
grows on the trees.

Each year, I wait for autumn.

Walk

It's going to be warmer than usual
tonight.

By the side of a Connemara road,
the dandelions
are ghosts now, soft white spheres
waiting to be blown away
and reborn.

By the side of a Connemara road,
the buttercups
slenderly rise above
the swaying grass; each tiny yellow flower
is a little note
of music.

*

It's evening, and
in the middle of a Connemara road, the sun
is caught
in those bits of stone
beneath the tarmac; orange shards
lead on towards Renvyle.

It's evening, and
the air above
this Connemara road
is playing host
to parties of midges: chaotic swirls
of grey-brown specks.

I think
tonight
is going to be warmer
than usual.

Memory of dancing

I
Clouds stepped across
the dance floor
or seemed to—their shadows
light.

That's because
the dance floor
was our patio—lit beneath
glittering balls
of leaves
on trees,

the dying sun alive
on green ovals.

II
Our feet
were little creatures
that didn't know
the way,

scampering forward
and retreating.

But the music
went on
and so we did,

MEMORY OF DANCING

bending towards each other
like kissing daffodils—

all snout,

but, my God,
surely pretty.

Notes

Many thanks to my dear friends John Douglas and Eamon Grennan, for years of advice both heeded and naively ignored. Special thanks to Eamon for helping finalise this collection. Thanks also to my editor and collaborator now on three projects, Katherine Farmar, and to Anna and Tony Farmar for continuing to legitimise my ramblings.

All of the poems here originally appeared (either in earlier or their current forms) in a small magazine I edited for over ten years, *Totally Fushed*.

'Through the Raindrops' was inspired by the video for Michael Jackson's 'Stranger in Moscow', directed by Nick Brandt.